My Grandma and Grandpa

By Jenny Giles
Photographs by Lindsay Edwards

I am going to stay

with Grandma and Grandpa.

My mom and dad

are going away for two days.

3

I like staying with Grandma and Grandpa.

My pajamas and my toothbrush are in my bag.
My teddy is in my bag, too.

5

Grandma is good at cooking.

I like helping her.

7

Grandma makes cupcakes

for all of us.

We like eating Grandma's cupcakes.

9

Grandpa plays soccer with me.

He is good at soccer.

I can run and kick the ball to Grandpa.

11

We make houses with cards.

We make big houses and little houses.

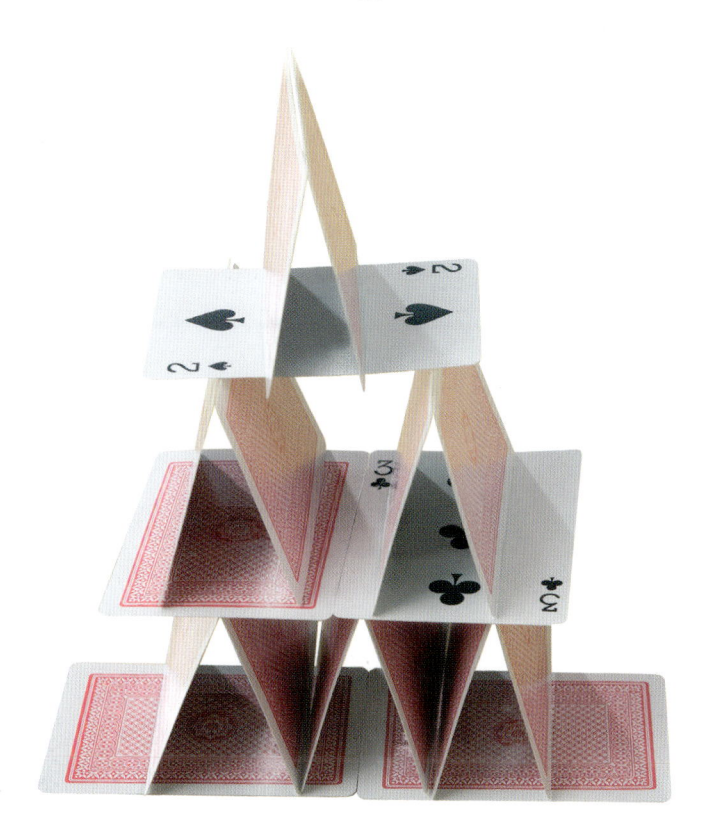

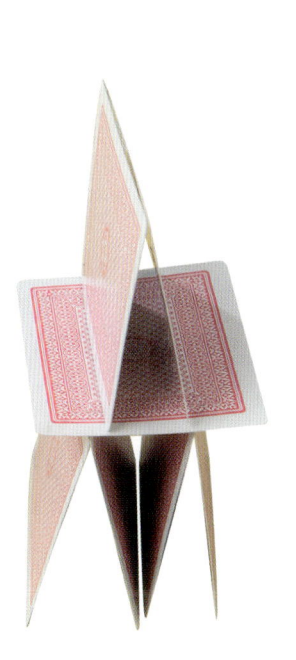

This is where I sleep

at Grandma and Grandpa's house.

My toys are in a box.

Can you see the photo of me?

15

My grandma and grandpa love me.

They like looking after me.